I0151574

FLUSH IT
and
Go With the Flow

World rights reserved. This book or any portion thereof may not be copied or reproduced in any form or manner whatever, except as provided by law, without the written permission of the publisher, except by a reviewer who may quote brief passages in a review

The author assumes full responsibility for the accuracy of all facts and quotations as cited in this book. The opinions expressed in this book are the author's personal views andinterpretations, and do not necessarily reflect those of the publisher.

This book is provided with the understanding that the publisher is not engaged in giving spiritual, legal, medical, or other professional advice. If authoritative advice is needed, the reader should seek the counsel of a competent professional.

Copyright © 2018 TEACH Services, Inc.

ISBN-13: 978-1-4796-0876-8 (Paperback)

ISBN-13: 978-1-4796-0877-5 (ePub)

ISBN-13: 978-1-4796-0878-2 (Mobi)

TEACH Services, Inc.
PUBLISHING
www.TEACHServices.com • (800) 367-1844

Wellness Coaches

- ◆ April Barnes

- ◆ Regina Bragwell

- ◆ Derick Carpenay

- ◆ Kimberly Chappell

- ◆ Elizabeth Goodson

- ◆ Hunt Hudson

- ◆ James Kendrick

- ◆ Dion Lucas

- ◆ Daniel Luttrell

- ◆ Kevin Vickery

Emotional Constipation

- Don't Hold a Grudge

- The Longer You Hold on to Something, The Harder It Is to Let It Go

- Health Damages Can Occur

Everyone has the option to choose happiness. The longer a person holds on to grudges against others, the longer that person is going to be miserable. This misery not only affects relationships but also the grudge holder's emotional health, which in turn leads to a decline in physical health.

To Plunge or Not To Plunge

- The Choice Is Yours

- You Alone Have the Power to Plunge

- Closing the Lid Does Not Plunge Your Problem

When you choose to be happy and choose to forgive, you free yourself from emotional baggage. You can't expect to be rid of the emotional baggage by simply forgetting the issue; everyone must address the issue and release the anger. You may choose to resolve an issue with someone through conversation or by simply letting it go, knowing that you don't have time to allow that to impact you.

Where Did It Go?

- ◆   The Past Is Over

- ◆   Embrace the Present

- ◆   Move Forward to the Future

- ◆   No Dropping Turds in Others' Toilets

- ◆   Just FLUSH, FLUSH, and FLUSH

When you embrace the "now" and not the past, you can live life without emotional distractors. When there are less distractions in your life, you can give more to others. You can influence and inspire others only when you are free from emotional baggage. Many do not like being around negative people who zap their energy. Let go of the negativity.

When You Flush Too Much

- You Can't Flush All Your Problems Down at Once

- Life Does Get Backed Up

- Flush Frequently Over Time

- Don't Become a Party Pooper

With so many distractions in today's world, it is impossible to forget about everything. You will always face challenges, but it is important to know which ones to let go of first. The first problems you let go of should be the ones that impact you the most. If you learn to let go regularly, you will find more peace and not become a negative individual.

Sometimes You Have to Call the Plumber

- ◆ Mediations Are Necessary to Sort Through Life's Challenges

- ◆ Find the Right Plumber

- ◆ Allow Enough Time to Evaluate the Plumber's Work

- ◆ Stick With Him or Her and Accept the Outcome

It is essential to find someone who you can confide in on a daily, if not weekly, basis. You can't dump your problems on just anyone; you must find a person or a core group of people you can rely on each time you need to vent. Keep in mind that you may not always like what you hear from your "plumber," but always remember that this is a person you trust who is brutally honest with you.

Prairie Dogging

- ◆ Let It Go and No Take Backs

- ◆ Don't Hold It In

- ◆ The Longer You Hold It In, The Sicker You Become

Don't hold grudges. You will find that some people refuse to let go of negative encounters. You can tell who those people are over time because they are the ones who have negative attitudes and are never happy. They tend to be jealous instead of celebrating others. Be the person everyone looks to when they need to have a brighter day.

HIGH IN FIBER

Let It Go; Let It Flow

- Maintain Regular Maintenance

- Eat Emotional Fiber

- Take an Emotional Laxative

- Emotional Colon Cleansing is Good

- Renew Self Daily

- Overall Wellness Is Key

It is vital to maintain yourself. Yes, taking a shower is important, but that is not the only part of your daily maintenance. You must find a way to release negative energy whether it be through venting, exercising, meditating, or relaxing. If you do not take time for yourself, you are failing yourself and others around you. You have a purpose to fulfill that requires you to be at your optimal best each day.

Don't Just Spray Air Freshener

- ◆ The Issue Doesn't Go Away

- ◆ The More Air Freshener You Spray, The Easier It Is to Live in Your Own Stink

- ◆ Leave the Restroom With a Fresh Perspective

- ◆ Have a Clean Approach to Things

Saying that you have released emotional baggage, but you continue to let it destroy you, is like spraying a cheap air freshener in a port-a-potty on a hot summer day in south Alabama. If you hold on to an issue without releasing it, the problem is still there. You have to begin each day as a new day, and promise yourself that today is going to be a great day. Try to start each day with fresh perspective by convincing yourself that great things will happen. Challenge yourself to impact someone's life each day.

It's Not That Deep

- ◆ Drama Doesn't Solve the Problem—Remedy Does

- ◆ Crap Just Keeps the Toilet Clogged

- ◆ Call the Plumber or Fix It Yourself

- ◆ Save Money in the Long Run

Drama creates more problems. Many times just letting go of the emotional baggage can remedy the problem. Allowing hatred or hard feelings to fester tends to create barriers in your life which will eventually affect every area of your life from relationships to your physical well-being. When you experience conflict, think to yourself, "Is it really that deep?" Call your trusted friend—NOT everyone. You do not want to be labeled a "poop-stirrer.

TEACH Services, Inc.
P U B L I S H I N G

We invite you to view the complete
selection of titles we publish at:
www.TEACHServices.com

We encourage you to write us
with your thoughts about this,
or any other book we publish at:
info@TEACHServices.com

TEACH Services' titles may be purchased in
bulk quantities for educational, fund-raising,
business, or promotional use.
bulksales@TEACHServices.com

Finally, if you are interested in seeing
your own book in print, please contact us at:
publishing@TEACHServices.com
We are happy to review your manuscript at no charge.

www.ingramcontent.com/pod-product-compliance
Lightning Source LLC
Chambersburg PA
CBHW061417090426
42742CB00026B/3494